Cultural Conundrums

Poems on Inter-Connectedness

Matahari V.

First published in 2015
by Hansib Publications Limited

P.O. Box 226, Hertford, Hertfordshire, SG14 3WY
United Kingdom

info@hansibpublications.com
www.hansibpublications.com

Copyright © Matahari V., 2014

Cover photo by Avinash Pasricha
Back cover photo by Avinash Pasricha

ISBN 978-1-910553-19-0

All rights reserved.
Without limiting the rights under copyright reserved above, no part of this publication may be reproduced, stored in or introduced into a retrieval system, or transmitted, in any form or by any means (electronic, mechanical, photocopying, recording or otherwise), without the prior written permission of both the copyright owner and the publisher of this book.

A CIP catalogue record for this book
is available from the British Library

Production by Hansib Publications Limited
Printed and bound in Great Britain

Dedicated to the 'one' in everyone

The treasure of heaven hidden in the secret cavern like the young of the bird in the infinite rock

Rig Veda V 5.2. 5-9

Foreword

This book is about seeing the world with different lenses so that 'different' is not 'alien'.

The norms of the east and west sometimes bring about a clash of perceptions, create cultural conundrums. Much is lost in interpretation, much is misunderstood and walls emerge where a bridge could easily connect. Hence, we need to revisit the norm, redefine the boundary of tradition and modernity and reinvent systems that speak the common language of humanity.

Once again life strives to be born in spaces where it can breathe freely. Conundrums become abstract art from which each draws his/her conclusion. Consciousness unfolds. In these writings I try to garb myself in that shaft of light which peers through misty streets of misunderstanding and pathways of conditioned collisions to fragment the centred cohesive self. I gather these pieces and bring them to you. Between the rapture of dreaming bliss and in the throes of mortal life, love becomes a longing.

By dismantling fears, I reach the perennial in the ever changing landscape of a multi-dimensional reality. Like an infant looking at the infinite, beyond the prisoned womb of embodiment, I begin to understand a truth larger than myself. This is the truth of 'one' in everyone.

Matahari V.
(Mala V. Thapar)

for

His Holiness the Dalai Lama
Oprah Winfrey
Soli Sorabjee
Mrinalini Sarabhai

A special thanks to
Shri Avinash Pasricha for the pictures

Contents

PART ONE

Encounters	17
Doors	18
Ibsen's Doll House	19
The Human Touch	20
Dalit	21
Grace	22
Ifs and Buts	23
Horizons	24
Great Cosmic Dance	25
Phantoms	27
Name Tags	29
Faith and Doubt	30
In Essence	32
Crayons	33
Time stood still	35
Somewhere	36

PART TWO

Journey	41
Rent Happiness	42
Inevitable	43
Trapped	44
Recognition	45
And the rivers swelled…	46
Kadambari	47
Nevertheless	49

Guess Who 50
Hope 52
The New Year 53
The Unknown Friend 54
Transcendental 56

PART THREE

Flying Feathers 63
Wilderness 64
Essential Self 66
Uncensored Matters 67
The Sea 68
The Buddhist 69
Dreams 71
Temporal Time 72
Parallel Lines 73
Body, Mind and Soul 74
The Brook and the Mountain 75

PART FOUR

Till flesh gives way 81
Story of the Bird 82
Song of my heart 83
Rest 84
The Situation Room 85
Beyond Possession 86
The Mahabharata 87
The Bugle 88
I walk the night… 89
Silence 90
Illusions 92
Shadows 93
Thickets of Thought 94
Vow 95

PART ONE

"There are many humorous things in the world; among them the white man's notion that he is less savage than the other savages."

Mark Twain

Bharata Ratna M.S. Subbulakshmi
Photo by Avinash Pasricha

Encounters

when we meet
there is nothing much to say

i do not speak to reveal
the congealed blood of yesterday

you unfurl leaf by leaf
on this tree of life
turning my tomorrows into today

need i search for roots below
when they are cast in the mist above

i unclose my fingers, to reach beyond the fog
unfolding the adventure of consciousness
along the way

Doors

does every door open with a key
or is it sealed by individual perception?

where is the door to your heart
have you ever given it a thought?

whales in the sea, ravens in the sky
cross your mind
but never enter, why?

blue birds sing, woodpecker knocks
but the door to your heart is blocked
so happiness is a long way off

shut doors rust with time

the warmth of your hand
turns the knob of my shut door

gently opening it like fingers
reaching out to another land

Ibsen's Doll House

standing on the edge
she watched her wave crash

comforting shores were inviting
but misperceptions stood like rocks in the way

the doll house was the accepted norm
yet she escaped to find a new dawn
and refused to be a pawn

reaching out to greet the sky
she saw life pass her by

bare feet tread upon gravel and grit
and chiseled another form

life flew from muddy waters
to a new horizon

The Human Touch

if love makes us human
what do cultural differences make us?

if the first encounter is exhilarating
what does the last encounter look like?

some believe, others doubt
nestled in their midst,

do they see the tree or the forest
individuals or cultures?

does colour coding weave imperceptible designs
does fall determine your colour or mine?

is a conundrum a seasonal mist
baring fleshy trees in winter,
then cladding them in bright hues in summer and
fall?

is environment playing mind games
whispering sautéed thoughts amongst a medley
of colourful vegetables
in the heated pan of multifarious realities
seeking the fallible in the 'human'?

Dalit

shells strewn on sand
made my feet stumble
at your threshold

and when i opened my eyes
i became 'she'
'bliss' was the stuff that inhabited me

the nothingness of things, when all was gone
made space for another morn

the question remains
when all is lost,
what is forgotten
what is sought?
does one really have oneself
to clutch on?

Grace

anguished hearts
seldom look beyond narrow gates

enlightened beings always reside
in loving spaces that surround them

i span with my hands
every cubicle, every inch of mortal flesh

hoping to find molecules of a departed self
ice clinks memories of atoms
that energize with thoughts of 'You'

moments turn the hands of time
annihilating differences

and when history analyses events
in digitally fabricated hues
form and matter go unquestioned
as feet tirelessly prod the cobbled streets of yesterday

Ifs and Buts

if thoughts were trains
i would ride them
and travel miles without disdain

when the train would stop
i'd get down and talk
to the people around

if thoughts were ships
i'd sail them
under blue skies
in mellow waters

when rough winds
would blow my sails away
i'd look up at the heavens
and reach my bay

if thoughts were planes
i'd fly them
to fanciful lands
and meet and greet
my loves past and present

but thoughts are thoughts
so i turn to poetry and canvas
to create a world of sorts

Horizons

sometimes horizons are not far
our reach is not enough

our understanding, our circumstance
keeps our dreams asleep

around fires that slumber
 in conditioned beds
of yesterday's dictums

screaming sustenance over salvation
rigorously reminding riveting rhythms
of outdated mores that spiral and bind

freedom is not a flag to be waved
but an 'attitude' to cultivate

beyond the threshold of mime and dime
it is the pulsating rhyme of time

Great Cosmic Dance

then the storm became
a cyclonic surge of creativity

and reached out to an unseen God
then the blinds were drawn back
and the sun peered in
casting aside the dark

consciousness touched the hem of another dress
unbuttoning desire

some shrank back from shadows
others leapt forward to greet them

i stood still on that wondrous night
taking the wet with the wild

till the earth was soaked
and shoots burst forth

there was music
there was laughter
no fear of before or after

in this great cosmic dance
the lover within
danced with the lover without

twirling leaves around
swirling years ahead

i simply watched with wonder and awe

was this the chemistry
of the human and the divine

where were the defining lines
or were they even there?

i did not know
i did not care

the trees were bare
they held no snare

no charge for this cosmic fair
the spirit swirled and curled
vivacious and without form

no formality, no norm
one rhythm, one song

a cultural bonanza
aflame with eternal light

the evolution continues
though dancers change their garb

passion taps into territories forlorn
and emancipates the dancers as they dance on

Phantoms

i reveal myself
just as i said i would

and let you discover me
bit by bit, line by line
word by word

different shades of the rainbow
spell vibgyor[1]
as they ribbon the sky in geometrical design

from nooks and crannies
stories scream for an audience

while children sleep quietly wrapped
in the muslin of their dreams
awaiting arrival at different ports

shaking dust from weathered coats
worn by fractured circumstance

i bring you enchantment and laughter
from another land

and when you begin to unearth
the essentials
stories get swapped

---

1. Violet, indigo, blue, green, yellow, orange, red

some come from you, some from me
from the kitchen tables
where both humble and gourmet dinners lie

and hands meet along the walls
at strange corners of our existence

fleshing the spirit with a misty tomorrow
we travel time's train with laughter and sorrow

Name Tags

name tags hang loose
over your baggage and mine
as identification marks
in this world of sorts

we get pushed around
in the course of our journey

in steam trains
and fast flying planes

we wear masks that hide our fears
seek an identity in a storm and restitute in calm

when silence dwells, peace returns
still life paintings depict landscapes
unbroken by sound

deserts of desire, temptations and all
yet, Christ stands strong
amidst the jostling throng

Faith and Doubt

clouds don't complain
when moisture leaves them

the tree is unafraid of being disrobed by winter
nor fearful of its naked branches

they believe in the cycles of change
and adapt to the churning and burning of seasons
bleeding a profusion of colour

the tide turns for every man
nature blends benignly
man stalls at every bend in the road
afraid to be himself

is this Brahma's[2] design of augmenting creation
Vishnu's[3] way of sustaining it
Shiva's[4] mode of destruction of the redundant?

why then does man resist change and
crowd contentious selves upon 'simplicity'
obstinately standing in the way of evolution
only to be broken by age and wither away

why not surrender before all goes asunder?
does nature hear stories
embedded in layers of tumultuous minds?

---

2. Brahma is the Lord of Creation in Hindu Scriptures
3. Vishnu is the God of preservation in Hindu mythology
4. Shiva is the Hindu God of destruction

we offer gifts at shrines not knowing
if the deity really resides there
and not in the heart of a fellow brother
who has lost his sceptre and staff

while mortal children sort out mercenary marbles
in glass houses of illusory selves
priding themselves with possessions

Saudama[5] wonders if Krishna
would accept his humble offering of rice
and perhaps shower him with some lucky dice

like accessories deluding the self
lived and unlived moments sprinkle doubt

amidst faith and doubt
fate wrangles for space

in this race to find a new face
for 'freedom'
we find 'Grace'
in nature's ways

---

5. Krishna's childhood friend who had come to poverty and was urged by his wife to go and meet his King with an offering of some rice in anticipation his friend would reciprocate by ending his suffering

In Essence

in the folds of the petals
lies the essence of beauty

when the Indian summer turns to monsoon
and paper boats float in puddles
the rickshaw puller stands, waiting for the rider

who wears jasmine in her plaited hair
who sings softly in the tea gardens
plucking the aromatic leaves?

why am i lost amidst fields of famed irises
does the hour beckon me?

do i dream of riding the blue mountain express
in my India of various hues, fragrances and dialects?

when i sit on the charpoy[6] amidst fields of wheat
in my shaggy shawl with vermilion on my forehead

i know i have lived several lives
whose memory lingers like perfume
from distant lands

when bells chime
they call me to another place

then the white dove flies in the clear blue sky
i watch its flight with wondrous eyes,
struggling to free myself of mortal ties

---

6. Bamboo cot

Crayons

Crayons smudge faces with brown and yellow
white and black
lending complexion to the geographical patch

age is a great leveller
it crumples skin
and speaks but 'one' language
of experience and humanity

spanning across continents
age delivers unsought advice, to rustling feet
who have no ear for it

does grey reveal the years stacked away
is colour spiritual, material or intellectual
a ritual or a rite?

can the Shudra[7] win
the fight with a Brahmin[8]
in his circumstantial plight?

a commercial conundrum
speaks the mantra
'what's in it for me?'

interpretation begins to define destinies
ravens prey, where doves would fly

---

7. Lowly caste in India
8. Priestly caste in India

is transformation possible
when transgression is on its way?

is it heat, light or simply hindsight
or have we lost foresight
in this futile fight?

Time stood still

when love overflowed
time stood still

years of reckoning reality
brought silver to your hair and mine

moments froze in the hourglass
holding time tight

my heart leapt at your effervescent sight
was it an insight that flew my kite
to you that night?

Somewhere

somewhere along the way
walking the weather beaten streets

he stumbled into an alley
encountered a presence, felt a tremor

years rushed through wraps
till flesh loosened from bone
but he did not feel the years roll by

the 'moment' was all consuming
in its palm it held the quintessence
of a truth he'd long sought

it came to him at his journey's end
he caught at the string
to release mortality and transform reality

outside the window, cacti blossomed with red flowers

PART TWO

"The cup is not only the shape, the colour, the design but also the emptiness inside the cup..."

J. Krishnamurti

Shobha Naidu, Kuchipidi dancer
Photo by Avinash Pasricha

Journey

to and fro
from one location to another
quietly escaping crowds
we zone in and out of emotional landscapes

losing sight of here and now
building castles that will be washed with the first tide
we draw lines in sand that is neither yours nor mine

wondering all the while, how to make more
we get sore, sore, sore
the debris of yesteryears is no mean gravel
peeling the layers we lay bare our 'feigned' selves

and cry sometimes, at what we were
and what we have become
driven carelessly by
the tides of circumstance
not in control of ourselves

Rent Happiness

do we rent happiness
or do we own it?

do we tire of it
or does it leave us?

i wonder
at the blunder of humanity seeking the sought
trying the tried, reaching for the known

when the unknown vista lies in vestibules
behind closed doors that open with the memory key

and when memory tires, consciousness kicks in
then the seeker and the sought are one

Inevitable

there's an inevitability
about the syonni[1]
the anam cara[2], the soul mate

like the cool breeze on a summer evening
it feels your hair
blowing differences of
caste, colour and creed away

when we carry baggage of pretence
we tire
spontaneity dies a silent death

can cosmetic smiles create magic?
will 'Harmony' set the table for 'Peace'?

once again i feel a tingling in my fingers
the peacock inevitably dances
to the tune of the summer breeze

1. Soul mate in Panjabi
2. Soul mate in Celtic

Trapped

trapped in the web
of coming and going
being and becoming

the conundrum of leaving the land
without accomplishing the task

minds weave strands
of do's and don'ts
and crack under the pressure of external comment

the child within wonders how
coarse fibre gets entangled with fine yarn
weaving knots of a different sort

a potpourri of mixed identities
make identification a task

it's then that i turn to discernment
to find what is, and what is not

Recognition

you resided in the crevices
of my being much before
i encountered you

i loved you then
i love you now

and will do the same
much after you have gone

for love is a path i have chosen

have i become the rug
that touches soles?

though the lamp flickers
and the wind threatens

souls are warmed by those electrifying connections
that escape definition and division

strength surmises along twining vines
silence breaks into vibrations
resulting in emanations that mould human clay

once again it's Shiva's[3] cosmic dance
holding man in a trance

where shall i look
when 'He' has me in 'His' sway

---

3. Shiva is the great Yogi and one of the trinity of Hindu Gods

And the rivers swelled...

with the debris of yesteryears
and rain washed wanton fears

the Roman clutched his toga[4]
of several hues and commendations

seated amidst the privileged
he uttered knowledgeable words
turning to some, and away from the others

the scene has not changed much
classified and commoditised economically
some wrangle situations best
by ostracising and negating
while others stand by, and merely watch the play

is this just another way
of solving riddles
to let them remain unsolved

does life meander between stalling tributaries
awaiting permission to join the river?

or does the river need permission
to empty itself into the vast ocean?

why the conundrum
when the strand that unites is 'one'?

---

4. Oriental one piece dress like a flowing long garment worn by the Romans

Kadambari[5]

so you know...
Kadambari is 'she'
who is unafraid of revealing her true self
to those who know her not

the 'one' she knew all along
but never met
to him she was 'Kadambari'
and to him she spoke with candour

realising that fancy intersects reality
in a strange way

it was both Meera[6] and Radha[7]
in Krishna's[8] play

caricatures emerge in time
to meet a longing sublime

mystery unfolds the unfelt, the unseen
this is Krishna's 'leela'[9]
Dante's comedy divine

the Freudian slip
the cut and paste of internet lives

reference to the 'Sacred Feminine'
Da Vinci Code defines what is writ in time

5. Woman in Hindi
6. Krishna's devotee
7. Krishna's lover
8. Hindu God known for love
9. Cosmic play

different seasons sing to a different tune
how quickly they reveal change
breaking the solemn seal

no feathers are ruffled, no hours beckon
the responsible accept the 'yin' with the 'yang'

perhaps you will understand
this mix better than another

how she came to be 'she'
and he 'Him'
the fibre in each knew all along
while accidentally
pronouns slipped into sentences
unveiling gender

reaching 'Sushrut'[10]
bloodlessly dissecting experience
that lay embodied and cloistered
in the neurons of the human mind

---

10. Keen listener

Nevertheless

the saga continues
the 'jhankees'[11]
the crackers
the burning of effigies

it is Ramlila[12] played in the
'Parade Ground' in Kanpur
thronged with people of all ages

i watch the flame of diya[13] flicker
and the girl plait her long hair

i watch the myth unfold
and hear the cheer
of good over evil

and wonder
is it just Kanpur, India
or is it elsewhere... everywhere
that the battle of good and evil continues
through mythology and play?

11. Processions
12. Indian mythological tale the 'Ramayana'.
13. Lamp

Guess Who

it is evening and lamps hang low
on side streets covered with snow

soon the plough will clear it all
and erase memories steeped in gall
friends buried in the ground below

my thoughts resonate with
the icicles on the windshield
while driving on Highway 400
in a whirling snow storm

lights flash behind me
it is a cop car
"all well?" she asks
"yes, why?"

"you have your flashers on"
"yes" i say
"the road is slippery
and visibility very low"

i feel the highway and the storm rage strong

"it is Highway 400", she says
"you've got to keep moving
or you'll be run over"

i hit the peddle
tightly holding life
by the wheel
and steer my way

always aware of the shadow lurking near
while wheels skid on the snow below

i wonder if i can really speed
to match others on the road
and let the officer go

verily, verily, lights begin to show
a relief to be where one started

and then the flooding of consciousness
of what we consider 'home'
the officer, the guide
the snow storm
and the challenge below

Hope

hope crawls with tiny feet
through corridors of anticipation

here i linger amongst the burnt sienna of leaves
moist and anointed with rain

marigolds blossom, welcoming hope
awaiting footsteps, with baited breath

from distant horizons comes the wealth
of consciousness, awakening a new 'self'

spirits reach out to mend the punctured human fabric
and give another dimension to existence

hands that have toiled over many a soil
find a home in and beyond the twilight years

The New Year

you will never get it
if you keep throwing those
sacred moments of creation away

it's not about crossing time lines
it's about crossing mind sets
physicality follows when the spirit is in control

old wine spills into new spaces, as we celebrate
empty bottles get filled when 'saaki'[14]
clinks the glass to desire's brim

present moment is fashioned by past experience
once again she will speak a conceptual dialect
to many a passer by stepping in tomorrow

will she spell progress backwards
and fire shots that smoke the good with the bad

can peace enter through tight walls of prejudice?

can the dark cloud of gunfire lift the veil of misperception?

how long will 'Peace' stand, waiting its turn
when it is put on the back burner
and ego frontlines the barricade?

uncertainty troubles the human mind
more than the daily grind

---

14. Saaki is the bartender in Urdu language

The Unknown Friend

because this friendship was not tenured...
by external or internal limitations

it beckoned with open arms
and i ran into them

a truism called
speaking seeds of evolution

'must one walk into or away
from what one desires most?'
is the question life asked

i began to translate
response into karma[15]

and sands beat against
my breast tumultuously
battling desire with destiny

baffled i looked
far into the horizon
to the descending sun

and found my orange
merge with your blue

another time, another day,
washed the fear away

---

15. Deeds, duty according to Hindu religion

the ghosts of yesterday
arrived in the soft hands
of a new day

i still look for my lost self
in each grain
as i walk the terrain

fragmented selves lie buried in the sand
i try to bring together these pieces into a peace meal
and make them ready for the table divine

Transcendental

in each room of my life
i feel the presence of
your immeasurable self

people come and go as grains of sand
passing through the hour glass

another time, another day
just one more time, one more place

i become the vine and you the wall
i endeavour to climb

then the embers dissolve the heat
and as the burning logs fall

there is union of the satori[16]
and the zen[17]

the moon climbs the ink sky
igniting the landscape, with the indivisible
continuum
of 'siyoni' and the truth of 'unbridled love'

it rescues one from the tentacles
of an ever changing reality

i see people reach the point of beginning
at the end of their existence

---

16. Soul mate
17. Buddhist feeling of complete harmony

this is the wreath, the cross and the circle
whose circumference is never known
though its radius is measured

therefore, i say to you
you are not the one
but the 'only One'

and i look deep into your[18] soul...
to see the light of unmasked 'truth'

18. My beautiful mother

PART THREE

When asked "How do you pick up lepers with your bare hands?" Mother Theresa answered: "I see God in them, not the leper."

Mala Thapar in conversation with Mother Theresa

Malavika Sarrukkai, Bharatnatyam dancer
Photo by Avinash Pasricha

Flying Feathers

flying feathers don't make nests
adrift they wander
and lie in unknown lanes

sometimes unaccepted and alone
with energies that wane

when the emotional bank account is overdrawn
the red eyed craftsman
watches the birds gather grain once again

he is 'them' and they 'him'
in this becoming and being
they travel life's crowded lane of pain and gain

the question is not
'what is sane or insane in this winding lane'
but 'what helps us see the light within us'

Wilderness

leaves can't be pasted to a tree
like elicited responses
from continents far away

yet for some reason
i respect your 'naturalness'

it speaks humbly
of authenticity

i will not go to manicured gardens
that speak of contrived emotion
nor see lacquered faces masked with fear of revelation

nor to the land where blueberries grow
but you can't pluck them
and they dry on the vine

i love the wilderness of dreams that can be reached
here i chance upon spontaneity and a multicultural
dance of sorts

then rest my head on mossy stones
that deliver lessons of endurance

without regret i shall walk the unknown forests
stopping at brooks to quench my thirst

i wonder if there are such unmarked places left
in man's dig for commercial exploitation

and the savage in me wanders alone
seeking the unsought
loving the unloved

delving deep into life's mysteries
peeling the superficial mask

who am i and where do i go
do i need to know?

when the soul journeys
it does not seek directions
it operates on vibrations

and these sway the yellow gold
of fields where leaves fall

do lilies grow amidst snow?
does the winter rose fade
when frost settles on it?

i honour the seasons that bring your perfume to me
and when i look in your direction, i see a different reality

just like the lake Narcissus frequented
and the lake mourned the loss of Narcissus
not because he was handsome

but because in his eyes
the lake had found its beauty

I find 'myself' in seeking you

Essential Self

watered down by age
tranquil yet waiting to explode

any moment now, the trigger will go
and i will escape this man made show

any minute now my blossoming branches
will be dotted with red

and i will bend low to a lover's bow
then to the dance of different strokes

the charisma of connecting
is insightful and exciting

enthused consciousness begins to grow

Uncensored Matters

reveal themselves in little nuances
of daily living

the frozen smile
the occasional side glance

not 'when' or 'what' or 'who'
but the 'how' of it all cries attention

the 'how' of survival
the 'how' of sustenance

the 'how' of being
the 'how' of becoming
and transcending

caught in triangles
and parallelograms
of social rings

we rig the big picture
with flawed generalities

wanting the 'what'
without knowing 'how'

we tumble over our dreams
and circle the windmills
with unknown gusts of wind
that chime with time

she knits one plain, then one purl
until she reaches the moment sublime

The Sea

between the ruins
of two weather beaten continents
i am at sea

huge boulders of unbending wills
seek surrender from rolling hills

chipping away at their surface
with my bare hands

i discover that i have 'skin'
the enormity of the sea lies behind me then

i swim the strokes
and feel them befriend me

it's only when i cast fear away
that the boulders don't threaten anymore
as long as the shore is in sight
i'll swim with all my might

The Buddhist

"it was Him, wasn't it?"
no, "she", it was her

they fumbled over gender
two chimps first
then the two personas

grappling with the reality of
being and becoming
the seen and unseen

afraid to unveil, what lay buried deep within
they took cover, beneath Freudian sheets

souls softened with age, found utterance
from remote corners of extinguishing selves
dressed in sultry coats, carrying truths profound

cast in anonymity, happiness searched
for the 'enlightened way'
ignorance evaded it, seekers persisted
finding resonance and meaning in parley
in quiet, contemplative, meandering rivers of joy
under the 'Peepal'[1] tree, Buddha got this realisation
then wisdom burst and flowered from his two lips

before the bhikshus[2] joined Him
the world mocked the prince
carrying a begging bowl

---

1. A large leaf tree found in India, it is considered to be holy
2. Buddhist monks, followers of the enlightened one

after his revelation he became 'The Enlightened One'
so immersed was everyone earlier
in the conditioned conundrum of materialism

that 'one' got separated from 'every'
like a leaf from the tree

till the Buddha[3] under the Bodhi tree[4]
awakened to the new reality of discernment
and the middle path
then veneration followed

he had all those who mocked him, as his followers

---

3. Siddhartha the Indian prince who got enlightenment and started the religion 'Buddhism'
4. The tree under which Buddha got enlightenment

Dreams

dreams bought on credit
capable of everything that is impossible

can they forget the lone 'one' in the corner
the single leaf on the tree
holding on despite the cold wind

i wonder what strength keeps it going
when all have gone
who or what it waits for?

is it tenacity, affection, or the other
it longs for?

Temporal Time

the artist sometimes loses way and descends
on rusty benches, in front of stock exchanges
sometimes even scientists peer through
the wall of fame for a name

reality dawns when truth smudges pretence
creating spaces between shades of grey

when 'the blacksmith' forges iron
destiny moulds figurines that stay

is this the covenant of human effort
dreams either wither with time
or are realised in some way

what is adventure, but the streaming forth
of consciousness to new horizons
amalgamating new realities, with the old ones

Parallel Lines

not all lines intersect
some run parallel

not all angles are right angles
some are obtuse, others acute

not all lives end in Q.E.D.
some remain as unsolved theorems

we still keep chasing shadows
that escape our reach, as mist clouds perception

i wipe my eyes and then the screen
to determine where the rain comes from
and where the chips will fall

different colours make the rainbow beautiful
why can't individual differences do the same?

Body, Mind and Soul

the immigrant wondered as he landed
in this alien land, clutching his papers

he asked himself a simple question
"is the flesh arched to reach
the mind with innuendos
or is the mind pressured
with relationships fixed in time

does 'life' meander through time
or does 'time' meander through lives

is there 'space' for love
or does 'love' space out time?"

he walked this venue of jostling beings
in the fourth dimension

familiar faces wearing smiles like yours and mine
greeted him in this alien land of living and dying

here skin wrinkled before time, indented character
with experiential grooves

in the throes of fitting in
beauty of the body, mind and spirit
intertwined and knotted

once again, man stood naked before his God
his spirit yearning for union divine

The Brook and the Mountain

there's something in the brook
that is not on the mountain

there is gurgling laughter
that is contagious

there is water
that quenches thirst

there is humility
that enlivens the spirit

there's something in the brook
that's not on the mountain

yet people climb mountains to get perspective
then cage themselves in the ivory tower
and become the mountain they climb
and look below to all that is beneath them

all things look small
their perspective is lost in enormity

they claim their win
and are happy at their accomplishment

the brook smiles a 'knowing' smile
it has quenched many a weary traveller
and washed his tired feet

it is nestled beside a leafy nook
a haven to the forlorn
you may notice it or simply pass it by

a brook is a brook
a mountain just a mountain

PART FOUR

"To love is not to ask anything in return, not even to feel that you are giving something and it is only such love that can know true freedom."

J. Krishnamurti

Mallika Sarabhai in 'Unearthed' directed by Yadavan Chandran and produced by 'Darpana'
Photo by Avinash Pasricha

Till flesh gives way

she said: "how come you did not know?"
he said: "how come you did not see?"

regardless of differences, waves splashed endlessly
surrendering mortality to eternity, fantasy to reality

despite the wanderings in physical spaces
psyche never stalled or stumbled over distractions

when barriers dissolve and flesh gives way
who reckons the truth, who has the ultimate say?

when you are 'you' and i am 'me'
who are 'they' and where is 'hegemony'?

Story of the Bird

between this world and the next
there is a fine imperceptible line
i shall see one day

and somehow realise with the bird
it was futile to cry into deaf ears
that feigned affection

a felt impulse
cannot not be replaced
by a spoken word

quivering with fright
despite its spontaneous desire of flight
the bird retreated into the night

thinking she would never really get it right
so trapped was she by
vested perceptions and interests
that she lost sight of her flight

in a world that believed in 'might is right'
could she fly when her wings
were slowly being clipped by medicine men

'freedom before fall', was her message
but fall came before freedom was in sight

Song of my heart

"yes, i am hurting
from years arranged in array
uncovering debris of yesterday
unlived moments and footsteps that stray

into alleys hitherto unknown
to gather leaves that blow away

sea shells speak the language of another world
must i heed them and go?
dare i ignore them and stay?

as i parley with myself
i reach the unknown advisor within

he opens the door
i now know...and must go to another place... far away...

Rest

when the journey got tiresome
she turned to clean sheets
to introspect and throw her fears away

from the ajar window she perceived the world
dancing to different tunes

words she could not hear, reached her in visual images
torn across space and time
in symbols and signs

nothing can stop the endeavouring mind
from multiple lenses of imagination

she saw and heard life spring again
despite her physical inability to join them

it was not the end
but the beginning of
living life in another way

The Situation Room

i will come to you
and you must not resist the encounter
for circumstance lies in formatted graphs
on the architectural drafting board of time

am i designing the interiors for the exterior
or is it vice versa?

narrow spaces and urban characters
mired in fog, create conundrums

barbed wires enclose secrets
through this quagmire the pilgrim walks
wearing his thorny crown

does he dream of emancipation
resignation, reunion, rebirth or recreating 'Reality'?

if we are not self-aware and dare
we end up laying bare
our ignorant self in a defensive format

Beyond Possession

In some cultures 'yes' means 'no'
and 'no' means 'yes'
patterns emerge, shadows fall
on the crumbling wall

possessed with 'possessions'
stymied by 'stuff'
different cultures connect differently
in conference halls and shopping malls

or live in culturally exclusive pockets at St. Lawrence
Little Italy, Little India and Greek town, in Toronto

money changers tabulate the 'quantum leap'
pigeons circle skies strewn with myriads of technical
toys
then reach for the grain in the heap

it's to the earth that each returns
to the roots that fruit laden branches eventually bend

The Mahabharata

does 'Mahabharata'[1] ever end?
is Krishna still not the charioteer
the guide in times of trial?

what keeps realisation from manifesting itself?
must the heated coal burn
to give light
and waste away?

ashes remind me of sacrifices
that go unnoticed each day
gentle rain quenches the parched earth

Lucifer took his fall
so humility could take form
yet superficiality holds sway
and arrogance has hands of clay

---

1. A great epic of war in Hindu mythology

The Bugle

every heart has its bugle
every heart must play

to whose tune is the question
who will listen when he/she plays

such is the music
it rings in my y/ears

breaking infinite silence
with salty tears

I walk the night...

somewhere along the curb
i left my life
now when I turn around
it is hard to find

so, i carry on the tracks of time...
yes, i am walking besides the row of Ashoka[2] trees
lit by footlights in the dark

i am going to unfamiliar places
to meet unknown faces

somewhere on this journey
i pause in anticipation

somewhere on this journey
i encounter you

so engulfed am i
with the here and now
that love passes me by
and i do not know

---

2. Name of a shady tree found in India

Silence

"why are you so polite and impersonal Silence?
do sounds really hurt you?"

the long stretch of everlasting silence
like the vast expanse of an ocean replied

in 's i l e n c e ....'

now broken by the wispy winter breeze
carrying the bite of frost...
smashing 'sounds' silently
lives lost in your perpetual gaze...

waves crash to caress your shores...
smouldering fires quietly silenced...
carrying tales of woe begotten heroes

unsung and unheard of
kicking pebbles along the way...

while soldiers slay
silencing the noisy machine guns on their way

quiet mothers wait for footsteps with baited breath
truth is grey
a mystery, a well-kept secret
like mist on a winter's day

your walls have a seamless quality...
that seethes through the millennium like a rocket...
shooting stars, stopping at nothing
evading heavens in its array

ever wonder,
if God had something to say?

in the forest, in my closet, along the curb...
or somewhere in the cycles of birth and rebirth...

why did it not dawn on me
that silence was the message and also the way...
of the 'unknown' always

thank you 'Silence' for being polite and understanding
i am beginning to understand your 'scream' slowly...
i wonder if i will succeed

words drive me to distraction...
and colour my palette in an uncanny way

but if 'silence' be your wish, my friend
i shall paint its hue with grey
and learn its language of many dialects
to convey what words fail to say

and in its bosom will unfold
red cherry blossoms on the tree

then fingers holding a parasol will open gently
to shelter you from rain and hail some day

Illusions

life is brief and steals time away
it warms my heart
when friends call to say "hello"

like the cool breeze on the ocean blue
my heart lights up to you

it's neither yesterday nor tomorrow
but this very moment in time, that i borrow

from those tight corners stifling with hyper activity
it is here that i negotiate space

for life is on a leash and the string is being pulled
in different directions, in many a mundane way

will the buds unfold to flower
the spirit breathe into matter
through love's unknown streets

who will the lark sing for when the moon wanes
in the wee hours when the stars still shine

to whose delight will love abandon itself
if consciousness is constricted by shame and blame?

Shadows

undressing my soul
unafraid of the dark

i saw a shadow
peer through a crack in the wall

and i suddenly felt naked
it was 'I' looking at myself
like the picture of Dorian Gray[3]

the moment held time in its sway
the shadow did not age nor wither
it was waiting for the light to come on
before being dispelled into another world

in this illusive reality, we breathe
amidst falling and rising shadows we call our own
when all they are waiting for
is for the light to come on

---

3. 'The Picture of Dorian Gray' by Oscar Wilde

Thickets of Thought

sometimes when you can't reach me
you'll find me in the thickets of thought

here there are no boundaries to respect
no fears that attack
it is here that i plough and sow
it is here that i play and stay

when dictums dictate, there are diversions
to avoid their conversion and perversion
i stay as 'me', the observer and the observed

it is a fine rope, a thin line
straddling it is a challenge
yet it is the way

Vow

i have lived on the edge of the precipice
for some time now
and seen the precipice crumble

but i have not crumbled
just dug my heels deeper
into the quicksand of human relationships

then roped myself
holding on to a deep core within me
that does not quiver with the winds of chance

what will be, i do not know
what is, i care for
and spell each day with a Vow!

we don't build a future for our children
but our children for the future!